The European Union

Political, Social, and Economic Cooperation

THE
EUROPEAN UNION

POLITICAL, SOCIAL, AND ECONOMIC COOPERATION

The European Union

Political, Social, and Economic Cooperation

LUXEMBOURG

by
Rae Simons

Mason Crest Publishers
Philadelphia

Mason Crest Publishers Inc.
370 Reed Road, Broomall, Pennsylvania 19008
(866) MCP-BOOK (toll free)
www.masoncrest.com

First printing
1 2 3 4 5 6 7 8 9 10

Library of Congress Cataloging-in-Publication Data

Simons, Rae.
  Luxembourg / by Rae Simons.
      p. cm.—(The European Union)
  Includes index.
    ISBN 1-4222-0055-8
    ISBN 1-4222-0038-8 (series)
  1. Luxembourg—History—Juvenile literature. 2. Luxembourg—Description and travel—Juvenile literature. 3. Luxembourg—Social life and customs—Juvenile literature. 4. European Union—Luxembourg—Juvenile literature. I. Title. II. European Union (Series) (Philadelphia, Pa.)
  DH908.S56 2006
  949.35—dc22
                                        2005020732

Produced by Harding House Publishing Service, Inc.
www.hardinghousepages.com
Interior design by Benjamin Stewart.
Cover design by MK Bassett-Harvey.
Printed in the Hashemite Kingdom of Jordan.

Contents

LUXEMBOURG

European Union Member since 1973

Weiswampach

Troisvierges

Clervaux

Wiltz

Vianden

Hiederscheid

Diekirch

Reisdorf

Feulen

Ettlebruck

Grosbous

Echternach

Bettborn

Redange

Mersch

Graulinster

Saeul

Wasserbillig

Grevenmacher

Steinfort

Cappellen

Schuttrange

⭐ **Luxembourg**

Dippach

Hesparange

Bous

Pétange

Pontpierre

Remich

Differdange

Bettemourg

Frisange

Esch

Dudelange

INTRODUCTION

Sixty years ago, Europe lay scarred from the battles of the Second World War. During the next several years, a plan began to take shape that would unite the countries of the European continent so that future wars would be inconceivable. On May 9, 1950, French Foreign Minister Robert Schuman issued a declaration calling on France, Germany, and other European countries to pool together their coal and steel production as "the first concrete foundation of a European federation." "Europe Day" is celebrated each year on May 9 to commemorate the beginning of the European Union (EU).

The EU consists of twenty-five countries, spanning the continent from Ireland in the west to the border of Russia in the east. Eight of the ten most recently admitted EU member states are former communist regimes that were behind the Iron Curtain for most of the latter half of the twentieth century.

Any European country with a democratic government, a functioning market economy, respect for fundamental rights, and a government capable of implementing EU laws and policies may apply for membership. Bulgaria and Romania are set to join the EU in 2007. Croatia and Turkey have also embarked on the road to EU membership.

While the EU began as an idea to ensure peace in Europe through interconnected economies, it has evolved into so much more today:

- Citizens can travel freely throughout most of the EU without carrying a passport and without stopping for border checks.

- EU citizens can live, work, study, and retire in another EU country if they wish.

- The euro, the single currency accepted throughout twelve of the EU countries (with more to come), is one of the EU's most tangible achievements, facilitating commerce and making possible a single financial market that benefits both individuals and businesses.

- The EU ensures cooperation in the fight against cross-border crime and terrorism.

- The EU is spearheading world efforts to preserve the environment.

- As the world's largest trading bloc, the EU uses its influence to promote fair rules for world trade, ensuring that globalization also benefits the poorest countries.

- The EU is already the world's largest donor of humanitarian aid and development assistance, providing 55 percent of global official development assistance to developing countries in 2004.

The EU is neither a nation intended to replace existing nations, nor an international organization. The EU is unique—its member countries have established common institutions to which they delegate some of their sovereignty so that decisions on matters of joint interest can be made democratically at the European level.

Europe is a continent with many different traditions and languages, but with shared values such as democracy, freedom, and social justice, cherished values well known to North Americans. Indeed, the EU motto is "United in Diversity."

Enjoy your reading. Take advantage of this chance to learn more about Europe and the EU!

Ambassador John Bruton,
Head of Delegation of the European Commission, Washington, D.C.

Luxembourg's farmland

1 THE LANDSCAPE

In the northwest heart of Europe, just southeast of Belgium and wedged between France and Germany, lies the tiny nation known as the Grand Duchy of Luxembourg. Only fifty-one miles (82 kilometers) long and thirty-six miles (58 kilometers) wide, Luxembourg is slightly smaller than America's tiniest state, Rhode Island. Despite Luxembourg's small area, its 998 square miles (2,586 square kilometers) contain a surprising variety of landscapes, from forested highlands in the north to rolling farmland and world-class vineyards in the south.

QUICK FACTS: THE GEOGRAPHY OF LUXEMBOURG

Location: Western Europe, between France and Germany
Area: slightly smaller than Rhode Island
  total: 998 square miles (2,586 sq. km.)
  land: 998 square miles (2,586 sq. km.)
  water: N/A
Borders: Belgium 92 miles (148 km.), France 45 miles (73 km.), Germany 86 miles (138 km.)
Climate: modified continental with cool winters, warm summers
Terrain: primarily gently rolling uplands with broad, shallow valleys; uplands to slightly mountainous in the north; steep slope down to the Moselle flood plain in the southeast
Elevation extremes:
  lowest point: Moselle River—436 feet (133 meters)
  highest point: Buurgplaatz—1,834 feet (559 meters)
Natural hazards: None

Source: www.cia.gov, 2005.

FORESTS, HILLS, AND RIVERS

The capital, Luxembourg City, is located in southern Luxembourg and provides a cultural and political crossroads between Europe's great cities, since it lies 183 miles (294 kilometers) east of Paris, 118 miles (190 kilometers) southeast of Brussels, and 110 miles (176 kilometers) west of Frankfurt. The rolling hills outside the city average about 900 feet (270 meters) in height.

Many people, including the residents of Luxembourg City, sometimes forget that more of this tiny country lies outside the city's boundaries. In fact, the Grand Duchy of Luxembourg has two distinct regions.

The rugged and fertile Ardennes Plateau lies to the north, accounting for about 68 percent of Luxembourg's area. Luxembourg's portion of the Ardennes is sometimes called the Eisléck or Oesling. At 1,823 feet (555 meters), this region contains the country's highest point. Medieval castles rise here and there between the thick trees. This region contains the Natural Germano-Luxembourg, a protected area that also extends across the border into Germany.

To the south are fertile lowlands, the Bon Pays, cut by deep river valleys. This region is also known as

The Moselle River runs between Luxembourg and Germany.

Gutland, the "Good Country." Luxembourg's farms and vineyards are found mostly in this region of rolling hills sprinkled with patches of woods.

Northeast of the capital is the Müllerthal Region, referred to as *Petite Suisse* ("Little Switzerland") because of the area's rugged rocks. These rocks stand amid thick forests, their fantastic natural formations offering hikers twisting paths that climb between moss-covered stones. Just east of the capital is Luxembourg's portion of the Moselle Valley, known for its vineyards. At Luxembourg's southernmost end, a narrow swath of ruddy soil, known as the *Minette* or the "Land

Luxembourg's Petite Suisse

of the Red Earth," is a reminder of the country's once vast deposits of iron ore.

Luxembourg's four most important rivers are the Alzette, the Moselle, the Our, and the Sauer, but many smaller streams and channels also wind through Luxembourg's forests. Most of the rivers drain into the Sauer, which in turn flows into the Moselle River along the country's eastern border. The Moselle River was canalized in 1964, so that today it links the Grand Duchy to larger European waterways.

A MILD CLIMATE

In a country this small, the climate doesn't vary much from one end to the other. Luxembourg enjoys mild temperatures most of the year, with warm summers and cool winters that rarely dip below freezing. The sunniest period is from May to August, when temperatures average around 68°F (20°C) during the day and 50°F (10°C) at night. April and September tend to be sunny as well, while November through February are the coldest months. The Ardennes Plateau often has snow all winter, when the sun shines only a few hours per day, but the Ardennes' high peaks shelter the land to the south from the North Sea's cold winds. Rainfall is spread out fairly evenly throughout the year; on average, Luxembourg has one good shower every three days.

FLORA AND FAUNA

One-third of Luxembourg is forested, providing home for many species of European wildlife, such as hedgehogs, otter, deer, and badger. The country is also a fisherman's paradise, since its lakes and rivers are home to trout, pike, eel, carp, pikeperch, and many other types of fish. The country's Petite Suisse region is a natural park that offers a safe home for wildlife.

Narrow hiking trails between rock formations in the Petite Suisse region

Like most European countries, Luxembourg has not escaped air and water pollution, especially around Luxembourg City. The areas of the south have also suffered from the booming mining industry of the past. As a member of the European Union (EU), however, the country participates in European initiatives to protect the environment, and it is working with the rest of Europe to clean up its land, air, and water.

Luxembourg's natural environment offers modern Europeans many recreational opportunities. In the past, the tiny nation's hills and forests provided the backdrop for a long and rich history.

Luxembourg's old city

2 LUXEMBOURG'S HISTORY AND GOVERNMENT

The Luxembourg national motto is: *Mir wölle bleiwen wat mir sin*—"We want to remain what we are." These words summarize Luxembourg's long history. Surrounded by larger nations, the Grand Duchy of Luxembourg has struggled to remain independent since the tenth century.

Luxembourg's Medieval History

Luxembourg, once part of Charlemagne's empire, became an independent state in 963, when Siegfried, count of Ardennes, became sov-

---

Who Was Charlemagne?

"By the sword and the cross," Charlemagne became master of Western Europe. Through his leadership, learning and order were restored to medieval Europe.

In 768, when Charlemagne was twenty-six, he and his brother Carloman inherited the kingdom of the Franks. Carloman died three years later, and Charlemagne became sole ruler of the kingdom. At that time the Franks were falling back into barbarian ways, neglecting their education and religion, while the Saxons of northern Europe were still pagans. In the south, the Roman Catholic Church was asserting its power to recover land confiscated by the Lombard kingdom of Italy. Europe was in turmoil—but Charlemagne was determined to strengthen his realm and bring order to Europe.

In 772, he launched a thirty-year military campaign to accomplish this objective. By 800, he was the undisputed ruler of Western Europe, a vast realm that encompassed what are now France, Switzerland, Belgium, and the Netherlands, as well as half of present-day Italy and Germany, and parts of Austria and Spain. By establishing a central government over Western Europe, Charlemagne restored much of the unity of the old Roman Empire and paved the way for the development of modern Europe.

Siegfried decided to construct his own castle on the original earthworks. This fortress, known as the Bock, became the foundation for Luxembourg City and is still visible today.

In 1060, Conrad, a descendant of Siegfried, took the title Count of Luxembourg. The land was a prosperous duchy (a domain ruled by a duke or duchess) in medieval Europe for nearly five hundred years. The dynasty founded by Siegfried produced some of the leading figures of the German empire in the fourteenth century.

By the end of the Middle Ages, most of Europe was fighting over Siegfried's city. Besieged and destroyed more than twenty times in four hundred years, each time it was rebuilt, its strength grew, until eventually, it become the strongest fortress in Europe after Gibraltar. In 1443, however, the duchy lost its independence when it fell under the control of the Duke of Burgundy.

ereign of *Lucilinburhuc* ("Little Fortress") after he acquired the fort from the monks of Saint Maximus Abbey. The refuge was situated on a Roman road that led into the valley, and the monks had built defensive **earthworks** there to protect the inhabitants of their estates.

Luxembourg in the Nineteenth Century

Over the next four hundred years, Spanish, French, and Austrian armies took turns occupying the fortified capital. Listed as a French forestry department

Historical drawing of the fortress of Luxembourg

during Napoleon's reign, in 1814, Luxembourg was included along with Belgium in the newly formed United Kingdom of the Netherlands. This state fragmented sixteen years later, when Belgium broke off from the Netherlands, taking half of Luxembourg along with it.

These years of political unrest fueled Luxembourg's desire for independence, and in 1830, the Dutch portion of what had been the Grand Duchy became present-day Luxembourg. The 1867 Treaty of London gave the entire land its independence. Soon after, the country declared

EUROPEAN UNION—LUXEMBOURG

itself neutral in international affairs. Luxembourg refused to be a battleground for international conflicts any longer. As a symbol of its determination, it set fire to its ancient and much-contested fort.

Despite the Grand Duchy's determination to remain neutral in European politics, the discovery of iron ore around 1850 pushed the country to the front-line of European economic influence. The tiny nation no longer had a fortress to inspire the envy of its neighbors—but now it had something far more important to contemporary wars: steel.

LUXEMBOURG DURING THE TWENTIETH CENTURY

Luxembourg's iron mines made it attractive to Germany during the first part of the twentieth century, and Germany invaded and occupied the duchy in World Wars I and II. The Luxembourg people resisted and fought valiantly to regain their independence.

After being occupied by the Nazis during the Second World War, Luxembourg decided to abandon its neutrality, and it joined various economic, political, and military organizations, including NATO and the United Nations. In 1948, the formation of Benelux—an economic union between

WHO WERE THE DUKES OF BURGUNDY?

For nearly one hundred years, the House of Burgundy was one of the most powerful in all West Europe. Its dominion stretched from the North Sea to the Loire and from the Loire to the Rhine, while Dijon, the duchy's capital, became an important center of both the religious and secular arts. Four dukes ruled at the height of the family's prosperity: Philip the Rash, who founded Burgundy's fortunes; John the Fearless, who engaged in feuds that almost destroyed it; Philip the Good (who may not have been so good, since he sold Joan of Arc to the English); and Charles the Bold, the richest of them all.

Belgium, the Netherlands, and Luxembourg—was an important step toward European cooperation that served as a model for today's EU. Luxembourg was a founding member in 1957 of the European Economic Community, which later became the EU.

By the end of the twentieth century, Luxembourg had developed into an active member of the European governing bodies, building on its reputation as having been one of the EU architects. The country is often said to "punch above its weight"; in other words, despite its small size, it has political power in the EU.

ON THIS SQUARE, ON 10TH SEP

THE PEOPLE OF LUXEMBOURG WARMLY WE

THE VALIANT SOLDIERS OF THE US 5

AND THEIR ROYAL HIGHNESSES PRINCE

AND PRINCE JOHN, HEREDITARY GRAND

ER 1944
ED ITS LIBERATORS.
MORED DIVISION
OF LUXEMBOURG
OF LUXEMBOURG.

GOVERNMENT

Luxembourg has a **parliamentary** form of government with a **constitutional monarchy**. Under the **constitution** of 1868, the grand duke shares **executive power** with the Council of Government (the duke's **cabinet**), which consists of a prime minister and several other ministers. The prime minister is the leader of the political party or coalition of parties having the most seats in parliament.

Legislative power is **vested** in the Chamber of Deputies; the deputies are elected directly to five-year terms. A second body, the *Conseil d'Etat* (Council of State), composed of twenty-one ordinary citizens appointed by the grand duke, advises the Chamber of Deputies as it drafts legislation. The members of the Conseil d'Etat are employed in regular jobs outside the government, but they are expected to fulfill their responsibilities as legal counselors in addition to their normal professional duties.

Luxembourg law, the judicial arm of the government, is a composite of local practice, legal tradition, and French, Belgian, and German systems. At the top of the judicial system is the superior court, whose judges are appointed by the grand duke.

POLITICS

National elections are held at least every five years in Luxembourg, and municipal elections occur every six years. Since the end of World War

The ancient stone walls of Luxembourg's original fortress.

II, the Christian Social Party (CSV) has usually been the dominant party in all elections. The Roman Catholic–oriented CSV enjoys broad popular support. However, in June 1999, national elections opened the door to a new government. For the first time since 1974, the CSV gave up its majority to the Liberal Democrat Party (DP).

The DP is a middle-of-the-road party, drawing support from professionals, merchants, and the urban middle class. Like other west European **liberal** parties, it advocates both social legislation and minimal government involvement in the economy. It also is strongly pro-NATO.

The Green Party has received growing support since it was officially formed in 1983. It opposes both nuclear weapons and nuclear power, and it supports environmental and ecological preservation measures. This party generally opposes Luxembourg's military policies, including its membership in NATO.

Luxembourg has come a long way since it was nothing more than a mighty fortress, drawing the envy of neighboring lands. Today, the tiny nation is a political powerhouse that plays a major role in the EU. Luxembourg's thriving economy is one of the major factors in its strength.

Luxembourg's farmland contributes to a healthy agricultural sector.

3 THE ECONOMY

Luxembourg's stable, high-income economy has experienced solid growth, low inflation, and low unemployment. Although Luxembourg, like all EU members, has suffered from the global economic slump, the country has maintained a fairly strong growth rate and enjoys an extraordinarily high standard of living.

Tourist literature often refers to Luxembourg as the "Green Heart of Europe," but its rural farmland coexists with a highly industrialized and export-intensive economy. Luxembourg enjoys a degree of economic prosperity almost unique among industrialized democracies.

Its industrial sector, once dominated by steel, has become increasingly diversified to include chemicals, rubber, and other products. Growth in the financial sector, which now accounts for about 22 percent of the **gross domestic product (GDP)**, has more than compensated for the decline in steel. Most banks are foreign owned and have extensive foreign dealings. About 2.5 percent of the population works in agriculture, while 14.3 percent work in manufacturing, and 83.2 percent in **service industries**. The economy depends on foreign and **transborder** workers for more than 30 percent of its labor force.

A STEEL FOUNDATION

In 1876, English **metallurgist** Sidney Thomas invented a refining process that led to the development of the steel industry in Luxembourg and the founding of the Arbed Company in 1911. This company is now the world's largest steel producer, and Luxembourg's iron and steel industry, located along the French border, is the most important single sector of the economy. Steel accounts for 29 percent of all exports (excluding services), 1.8 percent of the GDP, 22 percent of industrial employment, and 3.9 percent of the workforce.

The steel industry has changed over the years, however, and the metal is no longer as important to the world as it once was. The restructuring of the industry and increasing government ownership in Arbed began as early as 1974, and eventually led to the company's merger with two European steel giants, resulting in Arcelor, the world's most productive steel mill. As a result of timely modernization of facilities, cutbacks in production and employment, and a recent recovery of the international demand for steel, the company is again profitable. Arbed specializes in the production of large architectural steel beams; it also creates value-added products by recycling steel scrap metal rather than mining and producing new steel.

Luxembourg's government has also made wise decisions that have kept its economy healthy. When the steel industry slumped in the mid-1970s, the Grand Duchy reacted quickly by wooing big spenders from abroad with favorable banking and taxation laws. This prompt action allowed it to transform its economy from an industrial- to service-based one.

Luxembourg City draws tourists.

Nevertheless, the steel industry still plays a significant role within the principality's modern economy.

A Financial Hub

At the same time that Luxembourg's steel industry declined, the tiny nation emerged as a financial center. Banking is especially important: in 2000, Luxembourg had 202 banks, with 23,464 employees, and more than 14,000 holding companies. The European Investment Bank—the financial institution of the EU—is also located there.

Political stability, good communications, easy access to other European centers, skilled multilingual employees, and a tradition of banking secrecy have all contributed to the financial sector's growth. Germany accounts for the largest single grouping of banks in Luxembourg, with Scandinavian, Japanese, and major U.S. banks also heavily represented. These financial institutions' total assets exceeded $600 billion at the end of 2000.

Luxembourg offers a favorable climate to foreign investment, and over the years, its government has successfully attracted new investment in medium, light, and high-tech industry. Incentives cover taxes, construction, and plant equipment. U.S. firms are among the most prominent foreign investors, producing tires (Goodyear), chemicals (Dupont), glass (Guardian Industries), and a wide range of industrial equipment. The current value of U.S. direct investment is almost $1.4 billion, on a ***per capita*** basis, the highest level of U.S. direct investment outside of North America.

Quick Facts: The Economy of Luxembourg

Gross Domestic Product (GDP): US$27.27 billion

GDP per capita: US$58,900

Industries: banking, iron and steel, food processing, chemicals, metal products, engineering, tires, glass, aluminum

Agriculture: barley, oats, potatoes, wheat, fruit, wine grapes; livestock products

Export commodities: machinery and equipment, steel products, chemicals, rubber products, glass

Export partners: Germany 21.8%, France 20.1%, Belgium 10.5%, UK 9.3%, Italy 7.1%, Spain 5.6%, Netherlands 4.3%

Import commodities: minerals, metals, foodstuffs, quality consumer goods

Import partners: Belgium 30%, Germany 21.8%, France 12.5%, China 11.9%, Netherlands 4.5%

Currency: euro (EUR)

Currency exchange rate: US$1 = €.84 (July 8, 2005)

Note: All figures are from 2004 unless otherwise noted.
Source: www.cia.gov, 2005.

Driving through the Petite Suisse region

Foreign investors often point to Luxembourg's labor relations as a primary reason for locating in the Grand Duchy. Unemployment in 2000 averaged less than 2.7 percent. Labor relations have been peaceful since the 1930s. Most industrial workers are organized by unions linked to one of the major political parties. Representatives of business, unions, and government participate in major labor negotiations.

A Communications Center

Government policies also promoted the development of Luxembourg as an audiovisual and communications center. Radio-Television-Luxembourg is Europe's premier private radio and television broadcaster. The government-backed Luxembourg satellite company, Societe Europeenne des Satellites (SES), was created in 1986 to install and operate a satellite telecommunications system for transmission of television programs throughout Europe. The first SES ASTRA satellite, a sixteen-channel RCA 4000, was launched by Ariane Rocket in December 1988, and today, SES operates thirteen satellites. ASTRA 1K, the world's largest telecommunication satellite ever, was launched in 2003.

Agriculture

Luxembourg's small but productive agricultural sector provides employment for less than 3 percent of the workforce. Agriculture is based on small family-owned farms; most farmers are engaged in

Luxembourg's thriving vineyards

dairy and meat production. Vineyards in the Moselle Valley annually produce about 15 million liters of dry white wine, most of which is consumed locally.

Luxembourg's trade account has run a persistent **deficit** over the last decade, but the country enjoys an overall financial surplus, due to revenues from financial services. The small nation's healthy economy provides its people with a comfortable lifestyle.

A street performer in Luxembourg City

4 LUXEMBOURG'S PEOPLE AND CULTURE

A tiny piece of land squashed between larger neighbors, ruled for centuries by other nations, it's no wonder that Luxembourg's population today is about 30 percent foreigners, the highest ratio of any EU country. In earlier centuries, invaders swept across Luxembourg, vying for control of the prosperous and powerful little country—but today's foreigners cross the borders quietly, seeking employment opportunities rather

Downtown Luxembourg City

than military might. Luxembourg's per capita GDP was the world's highest in 1997, its standard of living consistently rates among the best, and its workforce boasts a remarkably low unemployment rate. These are powerful lures to people looking to create a secure and prosperous lifestyle.

Luxembourg takes a good deal of its identity from its neighbors' cultures. Its language, its food, and its traditions have all been influenced by the nations around it.

LANGUAGE

All Luxembourgers are **multi-lingual**, and many native Luxembourgers are fluent in four or five languages. Luxembourg children learn German and French beginning in elementary school, but they most likely speak Luxembourgish as their first language at home and while playing with their friends. Many also go on to learn some English, Dutch, Spanish, or Italian. Both the German and French languages are used in the press, in politics, and in daily life. French is most common in government and schools, though Luxembourgish is the language heard most frequently on the street. English is widely understood in tourist areas. If you visit Luxembourg City and enter one of the shops, you may notice that the shopkeepers automatically switch back and forth between several languages as they wait on foreign tourists.

FOOD AND ARTS

s cuisine is similar to that of allonia region—plenty of pork, fish, and game—but it also expresses the German influence in local specialties like liver dumplings with sauerkraut. Like its neighbor Belgium, Luxembourg's beers are excellent, as are the Moselle Valley's fruity white wines.

LUXEMBOURGISH

This Germanic language was adopted as the tiny nation's official language in 1984. It is spoken in Luxembourg, as well as in small parts of Belgium, France, Germany, and by a few descendants of Luxembourg immigrants to the United States. About 300,000 people speak the language worldwide.

Although Luxembourgish is very similar to German, it also borrows from French words. It is relatively easy for German speakers to understand Luxembourgish, especially when written, but more complicated to speak it properly because of the French influence.

Of all the EU member states, Luxembourg is the least famous when it comes to the arts and culture. Few Luxembourg natives are internationally famous in the arts, but Edward Steichen, a pioneer in American photography, is highly regarded in his homeland and among photography historians worldwide. Expressionist painter Joseph Kutter brought modern art to Luxembourg, and the sculptures of Lucien Wercollier can be seen in several public places.

And Luxembourg is working hard to enhance its reputation for art by building world-class museums and hosting fine arts productions. The main museums are in the capital city, where the National Museum of History and Art offers both modern and contemporary exhibits, with impressive collections by local artists, as well as a spectacular archaeology display. The permanent collection of the History Museum of the City of Luxembourg displays the thousand-year-old history of the capital of the Grand Duchy in an original multimedia and interactive manner. The Casino Luxembourg provides a forum for contemporary art.

Today, many native and foreign artists live in Luxembourg, including painters Jean-Marie Biwer, Robert Brandy, Patricia Lippert, Gast Michels, Moritz Ney, Marc Reckinger, Doris Sander, and sculptors Jeannot Bewing, Marie-Josée Kerschen, and Liliane Heidelberger. In June 2003, the Luxembourgish artist Su-Mei Tse won the Golden Lion, a prize awarded to the best national participant at the Venice International Exhibition of Contemporary Art.

Luxembourg is growing musically as well. The capital city's symphony orchestra has developed considerably during the past fifteen years, and its musicians enjoy a growing reputation for their musical quality. With the opening of the Philharmonie building in June 2005, the Luxembourg Philharmonic Orchestra (OPL) has at its disposal a concert hall that meets the highest musical standards. Opera also has its enthusiasts throughout the country. The Esch-sur-Alzette and Luxembourg theaters, as well as the Centre des arts pluriels d'Ettelbruck and the open-air theatre of the Wiltz festival, all provide inhabitants of the region with first-class opera productions. Rock music is well established in Luxembourg; rock'n'roll fans will soon have their own large, specialized concert hall in the south of the country. Music festivals through the spring and summer are helping to build Luxembourg's musical reputation.

The people of Luxembourg also have a passion for the theater, whether as spectators or as actors. Recently, open-air theater based on historical subjects has become very popular. Thousands of people attend these summer productions, performed almost exclusively by local amateurs. Unfortunately,

Say It in Luxembourgish

yes: *jo*

no: *neen*

welcome: *wëllkomm*

hello: *moïen*

goodbye: *addi*

thank you: *merci*

One of Luxembourg's shopping areas

Display by local artists

many Luxembourg actors and producers have had to leave their country to be able to support themselves with their work. Actors such as André Jung, Charles Muller, Thierry van Werveke, and Myriam Muller, and producers such as Frank Hoffmann have succeeded abroad while maintaining close ties with their homeland.

When it comes to literature, Luxembourg seems to be almost invisible. Partly, this is because its authors write in so many languages—German, Belgian, French, and English—that their works are not easily recognizable as Luxembourgish literature. Roger Mandersheid, a respected contemporary writer, often publishes in Luxembourgish. The people of Luxembourg believe it is only a matter of time before other Europeans discover their authors. The National Centre of Literature has been working for a decade, publishing a series of critiques on the great works of Luxembourg literature, to accomplish this goal.

ARCHITECTURE

Until the twentieth century, Luxembourg was a poor country, and its chateaux, manor houses, and rural churches reveal this fact. Only a few landholders could afford to build fortified chateaux such as those at Vianden and Bourscheid, and the abbey-church of Echternach is one of the few examples of elaborate church

QUICK FACTS: THE PEOPLE OF LUXEMBOURG

Population: 468,571
Ethnic groups: Celtic base, Portuguese, Italian. Slavs, and European (guest and resident workers)
Age structure:
   0–14 years: 18.9%
   15–64 years: 66.5%
   65 years and over: 14.6%
Population growth rate: 1.25%
Birth rate: 12.06 births/1,000 pop.
Death rate: 8.41 deaths/1,000 pop.
Migration rate: 8.86 migrant(s)/1,000 pop.
Infant mortality rate: 4.81 deaths/1,000 live births
Life expectancy at birth:
   Total population: 78.74 years
   Male: 75.45 years
   Female: 82.24 years
Total fertility rate: 1.79 children born/woman
Religions: Roman Catholic (predominant), Protestant, Jews, Muslims (2000)
Languages: Luxembourgish (national language), German and French (administrative languages)
Literacy rate: 100% (2000)

Note: All figures are from 2005 unless otherwise noted.
Source: www.cia.gov, 2005.

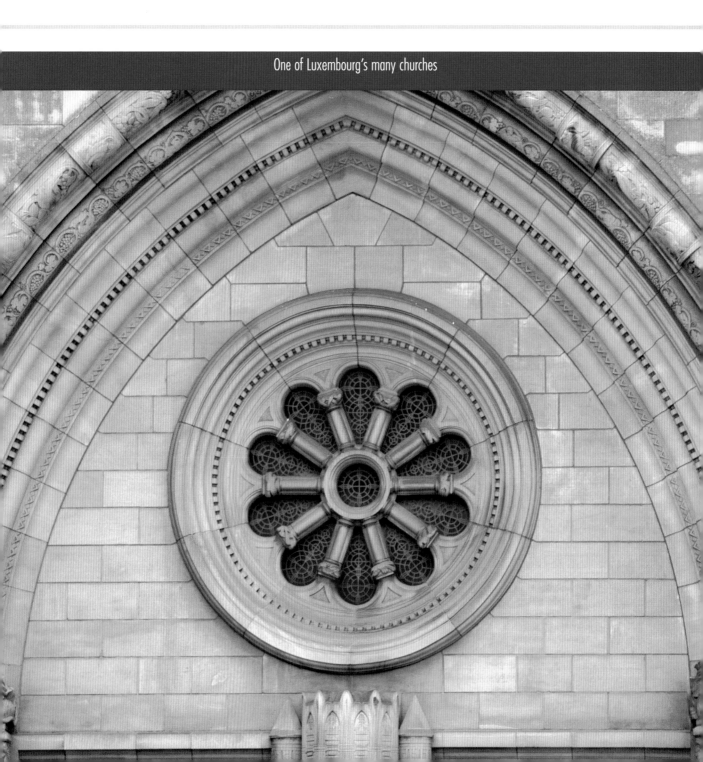

architecture in the country. In fact, only a few public buildings date back to before the seventeenth century. The old fortress town of Luxembourg, now part of the capital city, is on the UNESCO World Heritage List, and it offers a variety of styles of military architecture, dating from the Middle Ages to the first half of the nineteenth century.

When the Luxembourg fortress was demolished in the nineteenth century, new districts in the capital city were developed with the help of town planners. The Plateau Bourbon was entirely built in an architectural style that mirrored developments in Paris and Berlin around 1900, and the old forts were embellished with parkland. Civilian buildings of a monumental nature were constructed. The ideas of the German town planner Stübben influenced other districts. His plans included wide streets, the creation of public squares and green areas, and the development of gardens.

In the wake of the post-1985 economic boom, big banks, administrative buildings, and cultural buildings were built. During

LUXEMBOURG RELIGION

The country is almost entirely Roman Catholic. Many of the residents' most important celebrations are centered around religious holidays such as Shrove Tuesday, Easter, Ascension, Whit Monday, Assumption, All Saints' Day, All Souls' Day, and Christmas.

this phase of intense architectural creation, some projects were carried out by internationally acclaimed architects; the more recent include the MUDAM, designed by Ieoh Ming Pei, and the Philharmonie building by Christian de Portzamparc. During this period, purely Luxembourg architecture also enjoyed a new lease on life with leading-edge contemporary architectural projects and creations.

FESTIVALS AND TRADITIONS

Fifty days after Easter, a delightfully bizarre tradition is performed in the village of Echternach. Located on the eastern border of Luxembourg, Echternach is dominated by the Benedictine abbey of Saint Willibrord, first established there in the seventh century. Willibrord's remains are housed in the abbey's crypt, and the building is the focus of a dancing procession that's been performed for the past five hundred years or more. It may have begun back in the fourteenth or fifteenth century when people from all the parishes under the jurisdiction of the abbey would walk to Echternach during the Easter holidays bearing

Luxembourg is encouraging the development of its local artists.

their **tithe** offerings. These pilgrims would perform a sort of hopping dance as they proceeded to the abbey. This procession has been repeated through the centuries, and today it draws tens of thousands of spectators. Following a mass at the abbey, the procession of pilgrims dances through the streets of Echternach and back to the tomb of Saint Willibrord in the crypt of the basilica. The dancers "spring": two steps to the left, two to the right. The procession, composed of rows of five to seven dancers, each dancer grasping the ends of a handkerchief, moves forward slowly to the repeated strains of the trance-inducing melody, a happy but monotonous air that fades and rises. The musicians include brass bands large and small from across the country, accordionists, and sometimes fiddlers. The festival can last for hours.

Each August, the residents of Luxembourg City celebrate another sort of tradition: the *Schueberfouer* or *Fouer*, a carnival that is a descendant of an old cattle and flea market that once lasted eight days; today's fair is normally in town for about three weeks. Food and drink take center stage, especially *fouerfësch*, whiting fried in brewer's yeast, traditionally eaten with *fritten*

According to one legend, Laange Veith, the "Fiddler of Echternach," went on pilgrimage to the Holy Land with his wife, who died during the long journey. When he returned home alone years later, the relatives who had appropriated his property during his absence circulated the rumor that he had killed his wife, and they seized Veith, tried him, found him guilty, and sentenced him to be hanged. Asked on the gallows if he had a last wish, Veith asked for his fiddle. When it was handed to him, he began to play—and the townspeople who had gathered to witness his execution began to dance, controlled by a strange compulsion that lasted for as long as he played. Some of the villagers fell to the ground in exhaustion, but most were still dancing long after Veith, still fiddling, had descended from the gallows and vanished from town. It took the prayers of the great St. Willibrord, who hurried to the scene, to save the people from the spell.

(French fries), washed down with a beer or a glass of dry Moselle wine. The end of the fair marks the end of summer.

Wine growing is also important to the culture and traditions of Luxembourg. Grape festivals, usually held in October, are an opportunity to give thanks for a good grape harvest. Wine festivals are often held in the spring, in the assembly hall of the local winery or outdoors in a large tent. They feature dance music, traditional food, and wine (as well as beer).

Luxembourg's people and culture are sometimes hard to distinguish from the peoples and cultures that surround them. Nevertheless, this small but proud nation has a flavor all its own. One of the strengths of which its people are the proudest is the role it plays in the EU.

The EU flag

5 THE FORMATION OF THE EUROPEAN UNION

The EU is an economic and political confederation of twenty-five European nations. Member countries abide by common foreign and security policies and cooperate on judicial and domestic affairs. The confederation, however, does not replace existing states or governments. Each of the twenty-five member states is *autonomous*, but they have all agreed to establish some common institutions and to hand over some of their own decision-making powers to these international bodies. As a result, decisions on matters that interest all member states can be made democratically, accommodating everyone's concerns and interests.

Today, the EU is the most powerful regional organization in the world. It has evolved from a primarily economic organization to an increasingly political one. Besides promoting economic cooperation, the EU requires that its members uphold fundamental values of peace and ***solidarity***, human dignity, freedom, and equality. Based on the principles of democracy and the rule of law, the EU respects the culture and organizations of member states.

HISTORY

The seeds of the EU were planted more than fifty years ago in a Europe reduced to smoking piles of rubble by two world wars. European nations suffered great financial difficulties in the postwar period. They were struggling to get back on their feet and realized that another war would cause further hardship. Knowing that internal conflict was hurting all of Europe, a drive began toward European cooperation.

France took the first historic step. On May 9, 1950 (now celebrated as Europe Day), Robert Schuman, the French foreign minister, proposed the coal and steel industries of France and West Germany be coordinated under a single supranational authority. The proposal, known as the Treaty

of Paris, attracted four other countries—Belgium, Luxembourg, the Netherlands, and Italy—and resulted in the 1951 formation of the European Coal and Steel Community (ECSC). These six countries became the founding members of the EU.

In 1957, European cooperation took its next big leap. Under the Treaty of Rome, the European Economic Community (EEC) and the European Atomic Energy Community (EURATOM) were formed. Informally known as the Common Market, the EEC promoted joining the national economies into a single European economy. The 1965 Treaty of Brussels (more commonly referred to as the Merger Treaty) united these various treaty organizations under a single umbrella, the European Community (EC).

In 1992, the Maastricht Treaty (also known as the Treaty of the European Union) was signed in Maastricht, the Netherlands, signaling the birth of the EU as it stands today. ***Ratified*** the following year, the Maastricht Treaty provided f[
banking system, a common currency (
replace the national currencies, a leg
of the EU, and a framework for ex

The EU's united economy has allowed it to become a worldwide financial power.

EU's political role, particularly in the area of foreign and security policy.

By 1993, the member countries completed their move toward a single market and agreed to participate in a larger common market, the European Economic Area, established in 1994.

The EU, headquartered in Brussels, Belgium, reached its current member strength in spurts. In

© BCE ECB EZB EKT EKP 2002

200

© BCE ECB EZB EKT EKP 2002

100

© BCE ECB EZB EKT EKP 2002

50

© BCE ECB EZB EKT EKP 2002

The euro, the EU's currency

1973, Denmark, Ireland, and the United Kingdom joined the six founding members of the EC. They were followed by Greece in 1981, and Portugal and Spain in 1986. The 1990s saw the unification of the two Germanys, and as a result, East Germany entered the EU fold. Austria, Finland, and Sweden joined the EU in 1995, bringing the total number of member states to fifteen. In 2004, the EU nearly doubled its size when ten countries—Cyprus, the Czech Republic, Estonia, Hungary, Latvia, Lithuania, Malta, Poland, Slovakia, and Slovenia—became members.

THE EU FRAMEWORK

The EU's structure has often been compared to a "roof of a temple with three columns." As established by the Maastricht Treaty, this three-pillar framework encompasses all the policy areas—or pillars—of European cooperation. The three pillars of the EU are the European Community, the Common Foreign and Security Policy (CFSP), and Police and Judicial Co-operation in Criminal Matters.

QUICK FACTS: THE EUROPEAN UNION

Number of Member Countries: 25
Official Languages: 20—Czech, Danish, Dutch, English, Estonian, Finnish, French, German, Greek, Hungarian, Italian, Latvian, Lithuanian, Maltese, Polish, Portuguese, Slovak, Slovenian, Spanish, and Swedish; additional language for treaty purposes: Irish Gaelic
Motto: *In Varietate Concordia* (United in Diversity)
European Council's President: Each member state takes a turn to lead the council's activities for 6 months.
European Commission's President: José Manuel Barroso (Portugal)
European Parliament's President: Josep Borrell (Spain)
Total Area: 1,502,966 square miles (3,892,685 sq. km.)
Population: 454,900,000
Population Density: 302.7 people/square mile (116.8 people/sq. km.)
GDP: €9.61.1012
Per Capita GDP: €21,125
Formation:
- Declared: February 7, 1992, with signing of the Maastricht Treaty
- Recognized: November 1, 1993, with the ratification of the Maastricht Treaty

Community Currency: Euro. Currently 12 of the 25 member states have adopted the euro as their currency.
Anthem: "Ode to Joy"
Flag: Blue background with 12 gold stars arranged in a circle
Official Day: Europe Day, May 9

Source: europa.eu.int

Pillar One

The European Community pillar deals with economic, social, and environmental policies. It is a body consisting of the European Parliament, European Commission, European Court of Justice, Council of the European Union, and the European Courts of Auditors.

Pillar Two

The idea that the EU should speak with one voice in world affairs is as old as the European integration process itself. Toward this end, the Common Foreign and Security Policy (CFSP) was formed in 1993.

PILLAR THREE

The cooperation of EU member states in judicial and criminal matters ensures that its citizens enjoy the freedom to travel, work, and live securely and safely anywhere within the EU. The third pillar—Police and Judicial Co-operation in Criminal Matters—helps to protect EU citizens from international crime and to ensure equal access to justice and fundamental rights across the EU.

The flags of the EU's nations:

top row, left to right
Belgium, the Czech Republic, Denmark, Germany, Estonia, Greece

second row, left to right
Spain, France, Ireland, Italy, Cyprus, Latvia

third row, left to right
Lithuania, Luxembourg, Hungary, Malta, the Netherlands, Austria

bottom row, left to right
Poland, Portugal, Slovenia, Slovakia, Finland, Sweden, United Kingdom

ECONOMIC STATUS

As of May 2004, the EU had the largest economy in the world, followed closely by the United States. But even though the EU continues to enjoy a trade surplus, it faces the twin problems of high unemployment rates and **stagnancy**.

The 2004 addition of ten new member states is expected to boost economic growth. EU membership is likely to stimulate the economies of these relatively poor countries. In turn, their prosperity growth will be beneficial to the EU.

THE EURO

The EU's official currency is the euro, which came into circulation on January 1, 2002. The shift to the euro has been the largest monetary changeover in the world. Twelve countries—Belgium, Germany, Greece, Spain, France, Ireland, Italy, Luxembourg, the Netherlands, Finland, Portugal, and Austria—have adopted it as their currency.

SINGLE MARKET

Within the EU, laws of member states are harmonized and domestic policies are coordinated to create a larger, more-efficient single market.

The chief features of the EU's internal policy on the single market are:

- free trade of goods and services

- a common EU competition law that controls anticompetitive activities of companies and member states

- removal of internal border control and harmonization of external controls between member states

- freedom for citizens to live and work anywhere in the EU as long as they are not dependent on the state

- free movement of **capital** between member states

- harmonization of government regulations, corporation law, and trademark registration

- a single currency

- coordination of environmental policy

- a common agricultural policy and a common fisheries policy

- a common system of indirect taxation, the value-added tax (VAT), and common customs duties and **excise**

- funding for research

- funding for aid to disadvantaged regions

The EU's external policy on the single market specifies:

- a common external **tariff** and a common position in international trade negotiations

- funding of programs in other Eastern European countries and developing countries

COOPERATION AREAS

EU member states cooperate in other areas as well. Member states can vote in European Parliament elections. Intelligence sharing and cooperation in criminal matters are carried out through EUROPOL and the Schengen Information System.

The EU is working to develop common foreign and security policies. Many member states are resisting such a move, however, saying these are sensitive areas best left to individual member states. Arguing in favor of a common approach to security and foreign policy are countries like France and Germany, who insist that a safer and more secure Europe can only become a reality under the EU umbrella.

One of the EU's great achievements has been to create a boundary-free area within which people, goods, services, and money can move around freely; this ease of movement is sometimes called "the four freedoms." As the EU grows in size, so do the challenges facing it—and yet its fifty-year history has amply demonstrated the power of cooperation.

The EU believes that it can use its power to act as a "lighthouse" for the rest of the world.

KEY EU INSTITUTIONS

Five key institutions play a specific role in the EU.

THE EUROPEAN PARLIAMENT

The European Parliament (EP) is the democratic voice of the people of Europe. Directly elected every five years, the Members of the European Parliament (MEPs) sit not in national **blocs** but in political groups representing the seven main political parties of the member states. Each group reflects the political ideology of the national parties to which its members belong. Some MEPs are not attached to any political group.

COUNCIL OF THE EUROPEAN UNION

The Council of the European Union (formerly known as the Council of Ministers) is the main legislative and decision-making body in the EU. It brings together the nationally elected representatives of the member-state governments. One minister from each of the EU's member states attends council meetings. It is the forum in which government representatives can assert their interests and reach compromises. Increasingly, the Council of the European Union and the EP are acting together as colegislators in decision-making processes.

EUROPEAN COMMISSION

The European Commission does much of the day-to-day work of the EU. Politically independent, the commission represents the interests of the EU as a whole, rather than those of individual member states. It drafts proposals for new European laws, which it presents to the EP and the Council of the European Union. The European ssion makes sure EU decisions are implemented properly and supervises the way EU re spent. It also sees that everyone abides European treaties and European law.

EU member-state governments choose the n Commission president, who is then ed by the EP. Member states, in consultation the incoming president, nominate the uropean Commission members, who must approved by the EP. The commission is appointed for a five-year term, but can be dismissed by the EP. Many members of its staff work in Brussels, Belgium.

COURT OF JUSTICE

Headquartered in Luxembourg, the Court of Justice of the European Communities consists of one independent judge from each EU country. This court ensures that the common rules decided in the EU are understood and followed uniformly by all the members. The Court of Justice settles disputes over how EU treaties and legislation are interpreted. If national courts are in doubt about how to apply EU rules, they must ask the Court of Justice. Individuals can also bring proceedings against EU institutions before the court.

COURT OF AUDITORS

EU funds must be used legally, economically, and for their intended purpose. The Court of Auditors, an independent EU institution located in Luxembourg, is responsible for overseeing how EU money is spent. In effect, these auditors help European taxpayers get better value for the money that has been channeled into the EU.

OTHER IMPORTANT BODIES

1. European Economic and Social Committee: expresses the opinions of organized civil society on economic and social issues

2. Committee of the Regions: expresses the opinions of regional and local authorities

3. European Central Bank: responsible for monetary policy and managing the euro

4. European Ombudsman: deals with citizens' complaints about mismanagement by any EU institution or body

5. European Investment Bank: helps achieve EU objectives by financing investment projects

Together with a number of agencies and other bodies completing the system, the EU's institutions have made it the most powerful organization in the world.

EU MEMBER STATES

In order to become a member of the EU, a country must have a stable democracy that guarantees the rule of law, human rights, and protection of minorities. It must also have a functioning market economy as well as a civil service capable of applying and managing EU laws.

The EU provides substantial financial assistance and advice to help candidate countries prepare themselves for membership. As of October 2004, the EU has twenty-five member states. Bulgaria and Romania are likely to join in 2007, which would bring the EU's total population to nearly 500 million.

In December 2004, the EU decided to open negotiations with Turkey on its proposed membership. Turkey's possible entry into the EU has been fraught with controversy. Much of this controversy has centered on Turkey's human rights record and the divided island of Cyprus. If allowed to join the EU, Turkey would be its most-populous member state.

The 2004 expansion was the EU's most ambitious enlargement to date. Never before has the EU embraced so many new countries, grown so much in terms of area and population, or encompassed so many different histories and cultures. As the EU moves forward into the twenty-first century, it will undoubtedly continue to grow in both political and economic strength.

A bridge in Luxembourg City connects the city with the EU's complex.

6 LUXEMBOURG IN THE EUROPEAN UNION

Luxembourg has long been a strong supporter of European political and economic integration. In 1921, it helped form the Belgium-Luxembourg Economic Union (BLEU) to create an interexchangeable currency and a common *customs* regime. Later, Luxembourg became a member of the Benelux Economic Union and was one of the founding members of the European Economic Community (now the EU). It also participates in the Schengen

Group, whose goal is the free movement of citizens among member states. At the same time, Luxembourgers have consistently recognized that European unity makes sense only in the context of a healthy **transatlantic** relationship and have traditionally pursued a pro-NATO, pro-U.S. foreign policy.

Luxembourg is home to many important EU organizations, including the European Court of Justice and the European Court of Auditors. The Secretariat of the European Parliament is also located in Luxembourg, but the parliament usually meets in nearby Strasbourg, Germany.

Luxembourg took over the presidency of the Council of the European Union at the beginning of January 2005 for six months, the eleventh time since the founding treaties were signed that this responsibility rested on the Grand Duchy. During its presidency, Luxembourg hoped to pave the way for the ratification of the controversial EU constitution.

Luxembourg supports the EU's constitution—but not all the member states are in favor of it. The constitution covers many points, and many Europeans disagree with some or all of these.

One of the primary goals of the constitution is to prevent the EU from **encroaching** on the rights of member states other than in areas where the members have given their rights away. Critics of the constitution say that the EU can act in so many areas that this clause does not mean much, but supporters of the constitution say it will act as a brake to protect member states from a too powerful EU. At the same time, however, the

Luxembourg's EU complex

constitution provides for a greater role for the EU in more aspects of life. In some areas, the EU will have exclusive **competence**, in others a shared competence, and in still others, only a supporting role. The constitution also changes the way the EU reaches a decision, making votes dependent on a majority rule rather than a unanimous vote. Supporters of the constitution believe that if all twenty-five members had to agree, nothing would ever be accomplished. The constitution does, however, provide for an "emergency brake," whereby a country outvoted on an issue could take its case to the European Council. The voting system outlined in the constitution replaces the old one under which countries got specific numbers of votes. Critics of the old system objected that Spain and Poland had too many votes; they believe that the new method will allow for a fairer balance between large and small countries. The new constitution will also allow for the president to serve for two and a half years, rather than six months as is currently the case. Countries like Luxembourg that support the constitution believe this will allow the president to be a more permanent figure with greater influence and symbolism and the power to be more effective with greater continuity—but since the president will be subject to the council, the powers of the post will still be limited. Not everyone agrees, however.

Other key points in the constitution include:

- The commission, the body that proposes and executes EU laws, will consist of one national from each member state for its first term of

five years. After that it will be slimmed down to "a number of members . . . corresponding to two-thirds of the number of Member States," unless the European Council, acting unanimously, decides to alter this figure. It is felt that the current Commission is too big with not enough jobs to go round.

• The EU will for the first time have a "legal personality," and its laws will trump those of national parliaments. By having a legal personality, the EU will be able to enter into international agreements.

Luxembourg voters approved the EU's proposed constitution in a **referendum** in June 2005: 56.52 percent of the vote was in favor of the constitution, while 43.48 percent voted against it. Some 230,000 citizens went to the polls in the tiny duchy, where voting is **compulsory**. The vast majority of Luxembourg's politicians, the media, and the urban elite were in favor of the treaty and campaigned for a "yes" vote to prove the constitution could be resurrected. Meanwhile, French "no" campaigners had urged Luxembourgers to reject the treaty.

Luxembourg was the thirteenth country to ratify the constitution, but France and the Netherlands had earlier rejected it. This move on the part of the two larger countries threw into doubt the constitution's future, since it needs unanimous approval to take effect.

Luxembourg prime minister Jean-Claude Juncker said, however, that he hoped his nation's

Luxembourg is proud of its role in the EU

referendum would breathe new life into the constitution:

> It is the expression of the popular will of a small state but a great nation. This vote was every bit as important as those in France and the Netherlands. If Luxembourg had voted "No," Europe would be in an ultra-serious crisis. With this vote we are still in a crisis but a crisis which lets some signs of optimism appear on the horizon.

Only the future will reveal the path the EU will take through the twenty-first century. One thing is certain, though: Luxembourg stands posed to continue its role as a tiny but prosperous world leader.

A Calendar of Luxembourg Festivals

January: New Year's Day is a public holiday, celebrated much as it is elsewhere around the world.

February: The **Feast of St. Blasius**, celebrated on February 2, is a little like American Halloween: children go from door to door carrying rods tipped with little lights, called *Liichtebengelcher*, singing the song of St. Blasius—*Léiwer Herrgottsblieschen, gëff äis Speck an Ierbessen* . . . and begging for treats. This custom is called liichten (lighting). The song mentions bacon and peas, suggesting that long ago, the poor begged for food. Today, the beggars are children who eagerly accept handouts of sweets, although they prefer coins or a banknote.

Lent (Spring)

The Sunday after **Shrove Tuesday** (the first Tuesday after the beginning of Lent, the forty days before Easter, is **Buergsonndeg** (Buerg Sunday). In honor of this occasion, a buerg, a huge pile of straw, brushwood, and logs often topped by a cross, becomes a roaring bonfire. At the hour appointed for the spectacle, the pile's builders (usually the town's young people) march in a torch-lit procession to the site, their progress closely monitored by volunteers from the local fire department. A barbecue and mulled wine are available to provide spectators with sustenance and warmth. In some towns, the honor of setting the *Buerg* ablaze goes to the most recently married local couple. In ancient times, the blaze symbolized the driving-out of winter, the beginning of spring, and the triumph of warm over cold, of light over darkness.

Easter comes after Lent, a day of great celebration. According to legend, after the Gloria of Maundy Thursday mass, the church bells fly to Rome to receive a blessing from the pope. While the bells are away, on **Good Friday**, **Easter Saturday**, and **Easter Sunday**, the schoolchildren take over the bell's duties, calling the local people to church by cranking loud wooden ratchets, swinging rattle-boxes, and playing drums. The young racket-makers are paid in Easter eggs or coins, usually collected door-to-door on Easter Sunday morning after the bells have returned to the belfry. *Dik-dik-dak, dik-dik-dak, haut as Ouschterdag* (cackle away, today is Easter day) goes the traditional ratchet song.

In Luxembourg, as in many Christian countries, Easter would be incomplete without the Easter bunny and painted Easter eggs. Parents and grandparents hide Easter eggs around the house or the yard, and although supermarkets sell manufactured Easter eggs in industrial quantities, the practice of painting eggs by hand at home still endures. Social festivities take place on **Easter Monday**, not on Sunday. Many families attend open-air fairs.

April: Octave, during the second half of April, is the country's main religious holiday. Over a period of fourteen days, people from the countryside of Luxembourg (as well as from Germany, Belgium, and France) make pilgrimages to the cathedral in the Luxembourg capital. The tradition began in 1666, when the province of Luxembourg chose Mary to be the country's patron saint, calling on her to protect the people from the plague. Today, the pilgrims form a procession on the outskirts of the city, then proceed on foot to the cathedral. After devotions in the cathedral, pilgrims can obtain food and drink at the Octave market (*Oktavsmäertchen*). The Octave concludes with a procession that carries an ancient wooden statue of Mary through the capital's streets. Those in the cortege include members of the grand ducal house and representatives of the government.

May: May 1 is **Labor Day**, a public holiday when workers are honored.
Our Lady of Fatima plays an important role in the country's religious life. Since 1968, Her pilgrimage has taken place on **Ascension Day** (forty days after Easter) near the village of Wiltz.
On **Whitsuntide** (also known as Pentecost, fifty days after Easter) the usually bleak northern countryside of Luxembourg is transformed by the bright yellow of millions of tiny broom blossoms.
Gënzefest, held on the Monday after Whitsunday, includes a traditional parade, which celebrates broom and the customs of the old farming country.

June: National Day is June 23, the grand duke's birthday and a public holiday. The festivities in the capital begin with a torch-lit parade past the palace, where the people gather to cheer the royal family. Thousands then attend the *Freedefeier* (fireworks) launched from the Adolphe Bridge. Later, the capital gets into a party mood, with entertainment on every square: brass bands, musicians, and ensembles of every kind, clowns, mime artists, fire-eaters, and every possible kind of street artist.

September: Fair Day occurs each year in early September, a time for outdoor fairs, food, and fun.

November: All Saints Day, the first of the month, and **All Souls Day**, the second, are times to honor loved ones who have died.

December: There is no Santa Claus in Luxembourg at Christmas time (though the French Pere Noel sometimes makes visits), but **St. Nicolas Day** is celebrated on December 6. On evenings a week before this date, children put their slippers in front of their bedroom doors, expecting St. Nicolas to fill them with a small gift during the night. On the eve of December 6, children place a plate on the kitchen or dining room table that St. Nicolas fills with sweets and gifts. St. Nicolas also pays visits to children in schools.

75

Tripe
(Kuddelfleck)

This main dish makes four servings.

Ingredients
1 pound boiled tripe
2 eggs
sprinkling of flour, salt, and pepper
cooking oil

Sauce:
1 shallot
2 gherkins (small sweet pickles)
2 teaspoons of capers
parsley and chives
2 tablespoons of butter
1 heaping tablespoon of flour
2 cups broth or meat stock

Directions
Preparation of the sauce: It is best to prepare the sauce before frying the tripe, as it takes about twenty minutes to cook. Fry the finely chopped shallots in a little butter, and place to one side. On high heat, cook the butter and the flour until brown (you're making a roux), stirring often. Remove the pot from the heat and slowly add the stock, still stirring. Cook for a while longer, stirring occasionally. Add the cooked shallots and the gherkins, finely chopped, and the capers. Season to taste with salt and pepper. Add the parsley and chopped chives.

Tripe is available ready boiled at the butcher section of the grocery store. Cut it into rectangles. Then mix the eggs, salt, and pepper in a small bowl. Put flour in another small bowl. Dip the tripe pieces first in the egg and then in the flour. Meanwhile, heat the oil in a pan. Carefully fry the tripe pieces on both sides until crispy. When cooked, place the tripe pieces on a preheated plate covered with paper towels.

Serve with boiled potatoes.

Smoked Pork with Broad Beans (Judd Mat Gaardebou'nen)

Ingredients
fresh smoked ham
broad beans or other green beans
water
savory
1 onion, cubed
1/4 pound bacon
1 tablespoon flour
parsley
heavy cream

Directions
Soak the meat for 24 hours and then bring to a boil in the same water. Change the water after half an hour and add vegetables and bacon. When meat and vegetables are tender, add flour and cream and stir.

Green Bean Soup (Bou'neschlupp)

Ingredients
sliced green or wax beans
potatoes, diced
onion, chopped
4 slices bacon
1/2 pint cream or sour cream
sausage (optional)

Directions
Cover and boil in water until soft 2 parts sliced green or wax beans and 1 part diced potatoes and chopped onion. Fry 4 slices of bacon. When crisp, chop into small bits. Add bacon bits and fat to soup. Add the cream and simmer. Some people like to add a sausage to their green bean soup.

Gromper Keeschelche (potato pancakes)

This country's version of potato pancakes is delicately spiced with chopped onion and parsley before frying.

Ingredients
2 cups cooked potatoes, mashed
1 egg, beaten
1 small onion, minced
1/4 teaspoon salt
1/4 teaspoon pepper
parsley, to taste
2 1/2 tablespoons olive oil

Directions
Mix together mashed potatoes, parsley, beaten egg, and onion in a medium bowl. Add salt and pepper and stir thoroughly.

In a medium-sized nonstick frying pan, heat the olive oil over medium heat. Carefully place about 1/4 cup of the potato mixture into the frying pan, patting it into a circle about 1/4-inch thick. Fry until the bottom is golden brown and crisp.

Carefully turn the patty over and cook the second side until golden and crisp. Remove from the frying pan and drain on paper towels.

Serve with ketchup or salsa.

PROJECT AND REPORT IDEAS

Maps

- Make a map of the eurozone, and create a legend to indicate key manufacturing industries throughout the EU.
- Using papier-mâché, Play-Doh®, or flour and salt, make a map of Luxembourg on a wooden board showing the country's geographical regions.

Recipe for flour and salt dough:
4 cups flour
1 cup salt
1 1/2 cups hot water
2 teaspoons vegetable oil

Mix the salt and flour together, then gradually add the water until the dough becomes elastic. If your mixture turns out too sticky, simply add more flour. If it turns out too crumbly, simply add more water. Knead the dough until it's a good consistency. If you want colored dough, mix food coloring into the water before adding it to the dry ingredients. Or you can paint your creation after baking it at 200°F (93°C) for one hour.

Written Reports

- Choose someone from Luxembourg's past to be your pen pal. Write a letter to your pen pal; what questions will you want to include about their lives? What do you think they would be interested in knowing about your life today? Then do the research you would need to do to write a letter back from your pen pal, answering your questions about life in Luxembourg during her time.
- Write about the pros and cons of EU membership.

Oral Reports

- Research what you would see if you were a stranger walking down a street in Luxembourg during the Middle Ages. Describe for the class what you see, hear, and smell in as much detail as you can.
- Pretend to be a young person who lived during an earlier time in Luxembourg's history. See if your class can guess the period during which you lived simply from asking you questions about your life.

CHRONOLOGY

963	Luxembourg becomes an independent state.
1060	Conrad, a descendant of Siegfried, takes the title Count of Luxembourg.
1443	Luxembourg loses its independence when it falls under the control of the Dukes of Burgundy.
1814	Luxembourg is included along with Belgium in the newly formed United Kingdom of the Netherlands.
1830	The Dutch portion of what had been the Grand Duchy becomes present-day Luxembourg.
c.1850	Iron ore is discovered, pushing Luxembourg to the frontline of European economic influence.
1867	The Treaty of London gives Luxembourg its independence.
1868	The constitution calls for the grand duke to share executive power with the Council of Government.
1876	English metallurgist Sidney Thomas invents a refining process leading to the development of the steel industry in Luxembourg.
1921	Luxembourg and Belgium form the Belgium-Luxembourg Economic Union (BLEU) to create an interexchangeable currency and a common customs regime.
1948	Belgium, the Netherlands, and Luxembourg form Benelux, an economic union.
1957	Luxembourg is a founding member of the European Economic Community.
1964	The Moselle River is canalized to link Luxembourg to larger European waterways.
1984	Luxembourgish is adopted as the nation's official language.
January 2005	Luxembourg takes over the presidency of the Council of the European Union.

FURTHER READING/INTERNET RESOURCES

Barteau, Harry C. *Historical Dictionary of Luxembourg.* Lanham, MD: Rowan and Littlefield, 1996.
Eccardt, Thomas. *Secrets of the Seven Smallest States of Europe: Andorra, Liechtenstein, Luxembourg, Malta, Monaco, San Marino, and Vatican City.* New York: Hippocrene Books, 2005.
Heinrichs, Ann. *Luxembourg.* Danbury, Conn.: Children's Press, 2005.
Sheehan, Patricia. *Luxembourg.* New York: Benchmark Books, 1997.

Travel Information
www.thereareplaces.com/Guidepost/pdest/luti.htm
www.travelnotes.org/Europe/luxembourg.htm

History and Geography
reference.allrefer.com/worls/countries/luxembourg/geography.htm
www.lonelyplanet.com/destinations/europe/luxembourg/history/htm
www.rootsweb.com/~luxwgw/luxchron.htm

Culture and Festivals
www.lonelyplanet.com/destinations/europe/luxembourg/culture/htm
www.2camels.com/festivals/festivals_in_luxembourg.php3
www.yeworld.net/index/Culture/TA/EF/1258_2002126/158%2036%202002126110631.asp

Economic and Political Information
www.abacci.com/atlas/politics3.asp?countryID=353
www.eu2005.lu/en/savoir_lux/politique_economie

Publisher's note:
The Web sites listed on this page were active at the time of publication. The publisher is not responsible for Web sites that have changed their addresses or discontinued operation since the date of publication. The publisher will review and update the Web-site list upon each reprint.

FOR MORE INFORMATION

Embassy of the Grand Duchy of Luxembourg
2200 Massachusetts Avenue
Washington, DC 20008
Tel.: 202-265-4171
e-mail: washington.info@mae.etat.lu

Luxembourg Consulate General
The Luxembourg House
17 Beekman Place
New York, NY 10022
Tel.: 212-888-6664
Fax: 212-888-6116

U.S. Department of State
2201 C Street NW
Washington, DC 20520
Tel.: 202-647-4000

U.S. Embassy in Luxembourg
22 Boulevard Emmanuel Servais
L-2535 Luxembourg
Tel.: 352-460123
Fax: 352-461401

GLOSSARY

autonomous: Politically independent and self-governing.

blocs: United groups of countries.

cabinet: A group of advisers.

capital: Wealth in the form of property or money.

competence: Ability.

compulsory: Required.

constitution: The written rules and principles under which a government or organization is run.

constitutional monarchy: A political system in which the king or queen rules to the extent allowed by the constitution.

customs: Taxes payable on imports and exports.

deficit: The amount by which expenditures exceed income.

earthworks: Fortifcations made of earth.

encroaching: Gradually intruding.

excise: A government-imposed tax on goods used domestically.

executive power: The authority held by the person responsible for implementing legislative decisions.

gross domestic product (GDP): The total value of all the goods and services produced within a country in a year, minus the net income from investments in other countries.

legislative: The branch of government responsible for the writing and passing of laws.

liberal: Tolerant of different views and standards of behavior, and open to change.

metallurgist: Someone who studies the structure and properties of metals, their extraction from the ground, and the procedures for refining and making things from them.

multilingual: Able to speak more than two languages fluently.

parliamentary: Relating to a parliament form of government.

per capita: Per person.

ratified: Officially approved.

referendum: A vote by the whole of an electorate on a specific question or questions put before it by a government.

service industries: Businesses that produce and sell services rather than goods.

solidarity: Stand together in a show of unity.

stagnancy: A period of inactivity.

tariff: A government-imposed tax, usually on imports.

tithe: One-tenth of someone's income or produce.

transatlantic: Relating to crossing the Atlantic.

transborder: Crossing national borders.

vested: Having the unquestionable right to a privilege or possession.

INDEX

PICTURE CREDITS

Biographies

Author

Rae Simons has written several nonfiction children's books, as well as children's and adult fiction. She recently traveled to Luxembourg and enjoys learning about other countries and cultures.

Series Consultants

Ambassador John Bruton served as Irish Prime Minister from 1994 until 1997. As prime minister, he helped turn Ireland's economy into one of the fastest-growing in the world. He was also involved in the Northern Ireland Peace Process, which led to the 1998 Good Friday Agreement. During his tenure as Ireland's prime minister, he also presided over the European Union presidency in 1996 and helped finalize the Stability and Growth Pact, which governs management of the euro. Before being named the European Commission Head of Delegation in the United States, he was a member of the convention that drafted the European Constitution, signed October 29, 2004.

The European Commission Delegation to the United States represents the interests of the European Union as a whole, much as ambassadors represent their countries' interests to the U.S. government. Matters coming under European Commission authority are negotiated between the commission and the U.S. administration.